To:

From:

Caterpillar Kisses

Caterpillar Kisses

Lessons My Kindergarten Class Taught Me About Life

Christine Pisera Naman

DOUBLEDAY

New York London Toronto Sydney Auckland

PUBLISHED BY DOUBLEDAY
a division of Random House, Inc.

DOUBLEDAY and the portrayal of an anchor with a dolphin are
registered trademarks of Random House, Inc.

Book design by Caroline Cunningham
Caterpillar and butterfly illustrations © Louise Popoff

"The First Day of School" and "Snow Angels" previously appeared
in different forms in *Chicken Soup for the Soul Celebrates Teachers*
published by Health Communications, Inc., in 2003.

Library of Congress Cataloging-in-Publication Data
Naman, Christine Pisera.
Caterpillar kisses : lessons my kindergarten class taught me about life /
Christine Pisera Naman.— 1st ed.
p.   cm.
ISBN 0-385-51387-9 (alk. paper)
1. Kindergarten—United States—Anecdotes. 2. Kindergarten teachers—
United States—Anecdotes. 3. Teacher-student relationships—United States—
Anecdotes. I. Title.

LB1195.N36   2005
372.21'8—dc22   2004052726

PRINTED IN THE UNITED STATES OF AMERICA

May 2005

3   5   7   9   10   8   6   4   2

To my parents, Frank and Angie, who never stop giving and loving and listening (and listening and listening and listening). Thanks for believing in me. To say that I am grateful, to say that I love you, doesn't even begin to say it. But I am so very grateful and I love you so very much.

To Peter, my husband, I love my life with you. I love you.

To my children, Jason, Natalie, and Trevor, you are my world. My life began when you guys came. Oh, how much I love you.

To my brothers, Rocco and Dan, who are always there being just what brothers are supposed to be. I love you.

To my sister, Lisa, who is always there being just what a sister is supposed to be. I love you.

To Matthew, Diana, John, Nina, and Marissa. Know that I am always here and always loving you.

To Patty, who is an angel and a friend. Who made my dream come true first and keeps making time and believing in me. Promise me there will be iced tea some day. I love you.

To Bonnie, who is an angel and a friend. Who reminds me

it's okay to be me and reminds me that God is helping. I love you.

To Debra, who always had hope and whose words were so kind. I love you.

To Mel and Casey, my fairy godparents, who help me see God in everything. One day, God said, "Christine, this is Mel; Mel, this is Christine." I love you.

To Joan. Whose kindness and patience and love for *Caterpillar* made me love her.

To all the educators whom I had the honor to work with. I hope your memories are as sweet as mine. And even to those who I did not have the pleasure to work with. Know you are doing God's work.

To the parents, thanks for sharing your angels with me.

And especially to all of the caterpillars who allowed me to watch them wiggle into butterflies. Look back, I'm still throwing kisses.

Contents

Caterpillar Kisses

Introduction

I had not been teaching very long before I realized that amid the ordinary hustle and bustle of each school day, blessed little events, magical tiny moments, and lovely little coincidences were happening around me. I felt sure these happenings were heaven sent. I felt in awe that I was the only one (well, the only one over four feet tall anyway) to witness them. Because when they happened, it was always just my kids and me. I would wonder why I was blessed in this most special way.

These special moments would reveal themselves in many ways. They showed up through words, smiles, whispers, giggles, and even sometimes tears. However, no matter how they arrived, they always arrived through the children—through the precious, innocent little beings that I was honored to care for.

I called my children caterpillars because of the way they wiggled and wriggled their way through my door each August. They started off silly and unfocused, but then somehow without ever meaning to, through just the occurrence of growth, they became strong and sure just like butterflies. They wiggled in in August and flew out beautifully in June.

And when they left me, they left me with the most wonderful memories and the imprints of their kisses upon my heart. To me, the blessed little events, the tiny magical moments, and the wonderful quick coincidences were like kisses.

The only two things that I knew for sure when these amazing happenings occurred were that I was blessed by them and that I wanted to savor them.

But if you have ever been inside a kindergarten classroom, you know that five-year-olds live at a very fast pace that leaves little time for savoring and pondering. So, I kept a file card box on my desk filled with blank cards. And, as each of these wonderful moments occurred, I would savor and ponder as much as I could and then I would take a card and jot down a few notes in an effort to capture the moment.

I promised myself that when I had the time I would write them down to share with others. I would write them down to remind myself and others that within the most ordinary day God's love is ever present and shining bright.

On my final day as a teacher, I walked out of the classroom for the last time holding a full card box. A box full of caterpillar kisses. The next day I opened the box, took out a card, and began to write.

1

August

The First Day of School

It was the first day of school, the first hour to be exact, and I sat at my desk in the front of the room surveying the class before me. The motley crew of five-year-olds scattered in front of me comprised this year's kindergarten class. The names and faces change from year to year. They are boys and girls, tall and short, plump and thin. They are blonde and brunette and one is always a redhead. Their hair is short and long. Their uniforms are neatly pressed and wrinkled. They come bearing everything but the kitchen sink and they come empty handed. They are always very different from, yet very similar to, last year's class. They are also very different from, yet very similar to, one another. However, although each comes in a unique outer wrapping, inside they are all five-year-olds. And I have always found five-year-olds to be a very good thing.

They sat before me, each coloring a paper caterpillar with their name printed on it. This was one of my favorite "getting to know you" activities. I have found through the years that there is nothing children enjoy more than seeing their name anywhere and everywhere. Printed big, bright, and bold. They enjoy it; they become flattered and proud. "If my name is here, I must belong," their eyes seem to say.

I studied them with interest, noting how uniquely they approached the task assigned to them. Some sat straight and tall, coloring perfectly and confidently inside the lines as if they were modeling for a Norman Rockwell painting, while others looked more like Spanky and the gang from *The Little Rascals,* disheveled, slouching, and wielding each crayon wildly like a sword.

I rose from my desk and walked around the room offering encouragement with positive words and gentle touches on the shoulder. "These are simply the most beautiful caterpillars I have ever seen," I gushed.

As I continued to weave in and out of the desks, a clamor from the hallway drew my attention. Another class was passing by my doorway on their way to the gym. I did a double take as I realized it was not just any class, but my kindergarten class from last year—this year's first graders. I paused and watched as they scampered by, some of them waving. They had outgrown me. My heart melted and a lump formed in my throat as I watched them. A flood of memories washed over me. How they had grown! They had stumbled in last year so young, so insecure, with wide eyes and cowering shoulders. Throughout the year they had grown and by June their eyes had become sure and their shoulders straight. As the line of children dwindled, the flood of memories dried, leaving just a drop in the corner of my eye. I sighed and wiped the tear away with a quick hand.

"Teacher?" My thoughts were interrupted. Last year disappeared.

"Teacher?" persisted a voice from a straight and tall inside-of-the-lines colorer in the front row. "If we are caterpillars now," she asked, with her blonde ponytail bobbing, "will we be butterflies when kindergarten is over?"

I smiled at her as she tilted her head to admire her perfectly crayoned caterpillar. "Yes, Julie," I said, reading her name off the page. Her eyes darted to mine at the sound of her name. She smiled and blushed, surprised that I knew it.

"Yes," I said again, smiling to myself and enjoying the thought. I savored the image in my head for a moment longer; then, as the last first grader danced by my door, I said, "Yes, I believe you will be."

AUGUST: THE FIRST DAY OF SCHOOL

And with that, I somehow had a new understanding of the work set before me for the next ten months, the work that God had sent me to do.

Nurturing wiggling little caterpillars into beautiful baby butterflies.

2

September

An Apple for the Teacher

"It's for you," she said, boldly dropping a bruised red apple onto my desk. The apple wobbled unsteadily for a few seconds, then settled on its bottom.

"Thank you," I said warmly, peering into the part of her eyes I could see. Her blonde hair hung straight, covering most of her chestnut eyes.

"Sometimes haircuts cost more than the people in this neighborhood can afford," an experienced teacher once told me.

"That was very nice of you," I said, gently smoothing the hair away from her face. "I'll enjoy it with my lunch," I promised.

She stared at me blankly, then turned on her heels and returned to her seat. Only momentarily put off by her lack of reaction, I went back to my own work. But the strange silence that fell upon the classroom distracted me. I raised my eyes to find twenty pairs of five-year-old eyes staring back at me. I had no idea what they were looking at. I looked at them. Unblinking, they looked at me.

"They're waiting for you to eat the apple," said a voice that suddenly appeared next to me. It was the voice of Mary, who taught in the classroom next to mine. She had a habit of appearing out of nowhere. She would often startle me, as she did then. I would joke with her that she was always creeping up on me. I looked at her questioningly.

"They're waiting for you to eat the apple," she explained softly. "The teacher who had this job before you never would. She looked down upon these kids and their families. She didn't understand that dirty and poor are not the same thing. These people just don't have a lot of money. But it doesn't mean that they're bad or unclean. She said she'd never eat anything that came out of their homes. The problem is, the kids knew she said it and so did their parents."

I flinched, thinking it unbelievable that someone could have actually mouthed such words. Mary looked at me with a touch of sympathy in her eyes, as if she had just told me there was no Santa Claus.

CATERPILLAR KISSES

I guess she knew how naïve I was. She had been teaching in this school for twenty years. This was my first teaching job. And I came from the suburbs. What in the world did I know about the inner city?

I nodded at Mary. "Thanks," I whispered. I was truly grateful for her.

"You'll figure it out," she said, smiling faintly. That's something she said to me often. "You'll figure it out." Sometimes I knew what I was supposed to figure out. Other times I had no idea. She walked out of the room.

Twenty sets of eyes were glued upon me. For a moment, I stared back at them and then began figuring it out.

"Actually," I announced casually, checking the seating chart that lay on my desk. (Since it was still the first few days of school, I hadn't had the chance to learn all of their names yet.) "Actually, Rebecka," I said loudly, locating her name on the chart, "I don't think I can wait for lunch to eat this apple. I didn't have much of a breakfast, so I'm hungry. I hope you won't mind if I eat it now."

I picked up the apple. Overacting, I eyed it lovingly, then made a noise that telegraphed my longing.

They were mesmerized. Wide-eyed with anticipation, they awaited my first bite. After one last look, I closed my eyes and sunk my teeth deep into the apple. I chewed with my eyes closed, making grand noises of pleasure. Finally, swallowing, I opened my eyes to meet theirs still staring at me.

"Delicious!" I remarked. They bought the entire act. And loved it. Relaxed now, they shifted, giggling in their seats. They smiled at me and at each other. With the crisis passed, I pressed them back on track.

"You get back to your work," I suggested, "and I'll get back to mine." And that's what we did. They resumed their coloring, only raising their heads sporadically to watch me take my bites, which I dutifully did until tossing the core into the garbage can.

"Thank you, Rebecka," I said, as it plunked into the hollow metal can. Too shy for words, she just nodded with a delicate smile on her face.

The next day I found two apples on my desk. I ate them. The following day I found three, and the next day five. Somehow, I managed to eat them all. But by the end of the week there were seven. I was now in over my head and oddly wishing that at least a couple of them were oranges. But I guess nobody ever heard of an "Orange for the Teacher," so that was unlikely. It was getting tougher. I mean I like apples, but does anyone like them enough to eat seven a day?

The funny part about this is that the kids knew their apples, so it was impossible to fool them. Every day, each student bearing an apple would find their way to my desk and present their apple.

Then they would proceed to their seats and wait for me to eat it. As the morning drew on they would look back and forth from their work to me, waiting for me to choose the apple they had brought. I never even had to ask whose apple it was because as soon as I began eating it, the face of the child who had brought it would beam with pride.

After learning the hard way, and one day having to quickly gobble up three apples from 2:45 until the dismissal bell at 3:05, I learned to start early. So each day I began eating as soon as the first apple arrived. I munched through the Morning Prayer and the Pledge of Allegiance. I took bites during circle time and show-and-tell. I ate while doing paperwork at my desk, while teaching at the blackboard, and while offering individual help. I ate on my way to the bathroom, the library, and the cafeteria. There was no need for me to bring a lunch from home anymore. I couldn't possibly fit anything else inside my stomach.

One afternoon about two weeks after this whole thing started, I was glumly sitting at my desk gnawing on my third apple when Mary appeared.

"Hi," she said with a smirk. She had been enjoying my predicament.

"Hi," I answered back, trying to ignore her amusement.

"I just came by to see how your first month is going."

"Okay," I admitted, swallowing the last bite of the apple and tossing the core into the wastepaper basket on top of two others. "All except—" I stopped short, not positive I wanted to be that honest and not wanting to set myself up for more ribbing.

I looked at her. Her eyes were dancing.

"The apples," we finished together. Unable to control herself, Mary laughed heartily.

"Well, I guess if that's your biggest problem," she chuckled, wiping tears of laughter out of her eyes as she walked out of the room, "you don't have a problem at all." I wasn't sure that I agreed with her. "You'll figure it out," she assured me from halfway down the hall. Again, I wasn't sure I agreed with her.

It had gotten to the point where I would dread seeing them coming. As the school buses pulled up to the curb in the morning, I would look down from the second story window trying to spy how many of them were toting apples. Sometimes I could spot them right away clutching them in their hands as they hopped off the school bus. Often they would lose their grip and have to chase after an apple that was threatening to escape down the steep city street. Admittedly, I found myself wishing that apple "Godspeed," but my prayers always remained unanswered as those energetic five-year-old legs caught up with it.

Some days I was relieved, having only counted a couple of apples from the window. But I became instantly disappointed when the number of apples had greatly increased by the time the children reached the classroom, finding their way out of coat pockets and book bags.

Finally the breaking point came. It was a Tuesday morning. I had left my desk for only a moment to call on another teacher. When I left the room there were four apples; by the time I returned there were eleven. I just couldn't do it. And in spite of myself, I blurted out, "I just can't do it!" Startled, the children stared wide eyed at me from their seats. Realizing that that must have sounded much too harsh, I softened it.

"I'm sorry," I said weakly. "There are just too many of them. It's really so nice of all of you to bring me these apples. Really, it is. It's just that there are too many for one person to eat." They looked squarely back at me. Some of them looked angry; some of them looked crushed. Not one of them looked as though they understood. No matter what I had said, it was the wrong thing. The looks on their faces were unbearable to me. If I could have taken it all back and gobbled up all eleven of the apples, I would have done it in an instant. My mind raced, scrambling for a way to save this. Then I had an idea.

"There are just too many for one person to eat here at school," I clarified. "So I won't be able to eat all of them right now." I tested my words. "So I'll probably just be able to eat a couple."

"Which couple?" came a gruff voice from the back. It held a very wary tone.

"Yeah, which couple?" came a softer but no less accusing voice from the front.

"Well," I stalled, realizing I had stepped onto a land mine. "Well, that's the thing—I couldn't possibly choose between them," I said, beginning to recover. "Sooo, since they all look so good, I've decided to take one bite from each here at school, and then I'll take the rest of each apple home for later." I took a deep breath. Even though it was only a second, waiting for their reaction seemed endless.

Finally, someone said: "Ohhh, I get it, that's a good idea!"

"Yeah," someone else said.

"I get it, too," the rest chimed in.

I breathed a huge sigh of relief. They were satisfied. I was somewhat off the hook. All I had to do was take one bite from each, which I promptly did. No matter how many apples they showed up with in one day, I knew I could handle it now.

It was a solution. If only partly. It didn't solve the problem, but I figured it bought me time if nothing else, until I figured out the rest. I prayed for help.

Help came one Monday afternoon in the form of a four-foot-eleven-inch stocky Polish immigrant. I spotted her first out of the corner of my eye charging toward me across the parking lot.

School had been dismissed for the day. I had stayed late in order to catch up on some paperwork. The parking lot was pretty deserted except for my car and her, who, if I wasn't mistaken, had been leaning against the side of the building waiting for me. She wore a floral print housedress, black orthopedic shoes, and a babushka. As she crossed the parking lot, I was spooked by her sudden appearance and lost control of the eleven apples that were cradled in the bottom of my shirt. One by one, the bitten apples began to roll away from me. I scrambled after them, only causing more apples to fall out, until all eleven of them were rolling around on the concrete.

The woman came closer and scrambled along with me. While I stuffed them back into my shirt, strangely she was putting the ones she picked up into a colander. As I scrambled, I wondered if I was being mugged. Finally, with the apples gathered, we faced each other. Both of us out of breath, she mopped her brow and I blew my fallen bangs out of my eyes.

"Give me!" she ordered, pointing at the only two apples I had managed to gather into my shirt. Her thick Polish accent was evident. I recognized her as the grandmother of one of my students, but I wasn't sure which one. I was startled by her harsh manner and didn't know what she wanted.

"Give me!" she ordered again. Dumbfounded, I looked down at my shirt.

"You want the apples?" I asked, opening the shirt to show the bitten apples. I was embarrassed about what she could possibly think of me. What kind of person takes one bite out of ten apples? All of a sudden, without waiting for me to hand them to her, she reached over and snatched them.

"Tomorrow," she said gruffly. "Tomorrow I give you." She nodded firmly and turned away from me. I watched her walk across the parking lot and down the street holding her colander full of my apples.

———

The next day, a fresh-baked apple pie lay upon my desk.

"Wow!" I exclaimed as the children looked on. "Whose grandma did this?"

Kevin's hand shot up.

"Well, tell her thank you," I said. "And thank you to the rest of you too," I exclaimed. "This pie was made from apples from all of you." They beamed with pride.

"Thank you," I said with finality, turning back to the work on my desk. But once again, what seemed final to me was not to them. The weight of their eyes was upon me. I looked up to meet their stares. A hand went up. I nodded.

"Aren't you going to eat it, teacher?" he asked. If I hadn't been sitting down, I would have collapsed. Laughing heartily, I leaned back in my chair. They laughed along with me. I shook my head. I had no idea how I was going to get out of this.

"Mary!!!!" I bellowed. Mary appeared in my doorway like a shot. She was going so fast she slid to a stop by grabbing onto the doorframe. She was breathing heavily and her eyes darted around the room. I had never called like that before. She was certain there was an emergency. After scanning the room and finding nothing amiss, her eyes fell upon me. I was sitting in my chair grinning from ear to ear. Feigning anger, she made her way to me.

"What?" she asked, exasperated. "I thought someone was in trouble!"

"Someone is," I explained. "Me. Help." I pointed to the pie on my desk. "You said I could call anytime I was in trouble," I reminded her, doing my best to act pathetic. "They want me to eat it," I whispered, turning away from the children.

"So?"

"They want me to eat *all* of it," I explained. "*Myself. Now.*"

It was Mary's turn to laugh out loud. "Sounds like you have a problem," she said, teasing me. She turned on her heels and walked out of the room.

I sat back in the chair and closed my eyes.

"Teacher?" came the voice.

"Yes," I answered, willing my eyes open. I had no idea how to face this situation.

"Aren't you going to eat it?"

"Umm, well, umm, yes, of course I'm going to eat it," I stuttered, buying myself time. "Of course, I'm going to eat it. You see it's just that . . . I mean it's not that I don't want to eat it. It's just that . . ."

A clatter from the doorway drew our attention and saved me. Someone had placed something just inside the door and scurried away.

I squinted, rose from my chair, and went closer. I could feel my face widen into a smile as I saw what had been left. My problem was solved.

"Of course, I want to eat it," I called over my shoulder to my students as I bent to pick up my saving grace.

"I just need all of you to help me! I need you to help me," I called. "Because it's Friday." I laughed. "It's Apple Pie Friday," I hollered, holding the pile of paper plates and napkins high above my head. They cheered with delight.

And that is how Apple Pie Friday was born. They brought apples. Big ones, small ones, and every size in between. They brought them and brought them and brought them. They brought them on Monday. They brought them on Tuesday. They brought them on Wednesday. They brought them on Thursday. And on Thursday night I took them all home, got out my copy of Kevin's grandmother's recipe and made a pie.

That is how Apple Pie Friday was born. And that is how I (with a little help) figured it out.

CATERPILLAR KISSES

3

Lunch with Jesus

"Guess who I am?" he demanded, presenting himself before me. I turned my attention from the paperwork on my desk and looked directly at him. He looked exactly the same as he always did.

"Gee, Timothy," I said, looking him up and down, "I don't know."

Obviously, he was pretending to be someone other than himself. But, honestly, he looked the same as he always did at 8:30 in the morning. He wore navy blue uniform pants, a stiff white shirt, blue tie, and a navy cotton sweater. A school bag was strapped on his back and he held his lunch money in his hand. I furrowed my brow to prove that I really was trying, but shrugged and gave up. "Sorry. I just don't know."

"Okay," he said excitedly, enjoying our game. "I'll give you a hint." He paused a moment for dramatic effect, cleared his throat, bowed slightly at the waist, and said, "God bless you."

He opened his eyes wide and looked squarely at me. He waited for my reaction. I could tell he was trying to stay in character, struggling to keep the same gentle, serene expression on his face. Keeping my own jaw taut, I tried to stifle the smile that was threatening to break free.

"Umm," I managed thoughtfully, knowing full well who he was pretending to be. I thought it best that he tell me instead of me telling him. Finally, he couldn't take it anymore.

"I'm Jesus!" he squealed.

"Oh, I should have known," I said, giving the desk a gentle slap.

"For Halloween!" he clarified. "I know it's not until next week, but I wanted to practice."

"Good idea." I smiled.

"Thanks," he said, dropping the money onto my desk. He turned back quickly. "I mean thank you," he whispered with a slight nod, apparently deciding that "thank you" was much more Jesuslike than just a thanks.

"You're welcome." I laughed, glad there was only one way to say that.

I watched as he joined the activity of the children. He stopped each child that he happened upon to explain his newfound persona. They listened attentively. Then nodding with understanding, they carried on with their own chores. As with everything Timothy did, he did this with perseverance and passion. I watched him as he circled the room spreading his word to each and every one of his classmates.

As we carried on with our morning lessons and activities, he stayed perfectly in character, only forgetting on a few occasions. When he did, he adjusted quickly, overcompensating with an extra blessing or two. He spent his morning gently touching shoulders, nodding with understanding, and even hugging a few of his "flock" who seemed to need his extra compassion.

It was five minutes before noon, and Timothy was selflessly allowing the rest of the children to line up before him in the line to go to the cafeteria for lunch. It was then I thought that maybe I had better speak to him. Very possibly, this impersonation would not be as well received outside of our classroom as it was inside.

"Timothy?" I said.

"Yes?" he answered, raising his voice and cocking his head

up as if he was hearing a voice call to him from a distance. His posture suggested that he was standing before a crowd of thousands and he refused to make eye contact with me.

"Timothy," I said again, a touch more sternly. I think he knew by my tone that he had better acknowledge me.

"Yes, teacher?" he answered, still gazing into the distance.

"I understand that you are excited about Halloween, and it's okay to practice in our classroom, but I think you had better take a break from practicing until you come back from lunch."

I pictured the Sisters from the convent who served lunch being less than amused. He looked at me unconvinced, like I was spoiling his fun. But before he could protest, I said, "I think it's best." He dropped his head and stalled for a moment. But Timothy being Timothy, he was stalled for only a moment. He attempted to bounce back and raised his finger as if to introduce his next point. But I cut him short again.

"I think it's best," I said more firmly to let him know that I was not up for any more debate.

"Okay," he conceded, making a face and sighing. He let his eyes fall to his hands.

We walked the hallway to the cafeteria. I stopped at the doorway and let them proceed inside. Smiling at each and touching them gently on the back or top of the head, I bid them a good lunch.

Timothy, having stayed in his unselfish position in line, was last.

"Thanks, Timothy," I said, knowing that he would know what I was referring to.

He stopped, turned directly toward me, and much too serenely said, "You're welcome."

I shook my head and gave him a warning look. He was still in character and I knew it. But he also knew that "you're welcome" was still "you're welcome" so what could I say? He turned and passed me. I watched a moment more as he joined the class.

A couple of minutes later, after checking my teacher mailbox, I entered the solitude of the empty classroom. It had been a hectic morning and I was grateful for the quiet. I gently closed the door as if closing it harshly might somehow disturb the tranquility. I sat down at my desk and spread a paper napkin that had pumpkins printed on it in front of me. I laid out a turkey sandwich, an apple that was cut into quarters, and four Oreo cookies. At 12:05, alone in a deserted classroom with only the faintest murmur of children in the distance, this was a feast to any teacher. I closed my eyes, said a silent prayer, settled back in my chair, and with a relaxed sigh began nibbling on half of the sandwich as I read my first piece of mail.

Halfway through the page I began to relax and settle in. Not more than a minute later my peace exploded then disappeared with the sound of my name being barked over the intercom. With a jolt, the voice ordered me to report to the cafeteria. My heart skipped a beat. I closed my eyes, collected myself, and pushed away from the desk. The legs of the chair screeched against the linoleum. As I rose, Mary from the classroom next door popped her head through the doorway.

"I heard," I said before she had the chance to speak.

"Any ideas?" she asked, puzzled at such an unusual lunchtime interruption.

"I don't know what," I admitted, "but I have a pretty good idea who," I said, scurrying past her and out of the room.

Of all of the scenarios I had imagined on my way to the cafeteria, and there were many, I hadn't imagined the one I saw.

I paused for only a second at the entrance, spotting Timothy halfway across the room standing squarely center stage surrounded by five enormously displeased, crossed-armed, pinched-faced nuns. Scattered before him was spilled grape juice, a glass of water, crumpled white bread, and about a million goldfish crackers. It took me only a second to process the picture.

The Sisters' version: Timothy had committed the unforgivable. Timothy's version: he had simply turned water into wine, multiplied the loaves and fishes, and had begun feeding the thousands when I showed up.

I drew a breath, gathering courage; I cursed myself for not anticipating this and charged to the other side of the room. I growled as I broke through the circle that surrounded him. Without meeting the angry gaze of the Sisters that was now cast firmly upon me, I grabbed Timothy's hand, yanking him out of the crowd. I snatched the cup from his hand, spilling most of its contents. Then shoving the cup at the group of boys to his right, who I presumed were his disciples, I led him across the room with a tug. Timothy sighed, but knowing a protest would be futile, he let his hand melt into mine. We were halfway to the classroom before we started to breathe again. He peered up at me, waiting for my wrath.

"I think you better eat lunch with me today," was all I could muster. He nodded as a small satisfied and much too serene smile appeared on his face.

"Timothy!" I said exasperated, stopping short to face him.

"What?" he asked.

"You know what," I said a bit too loudly.

Thinking we were alone in the hallway, I was startled by the nun who was slowly, disapprovingly passing by us. I gulped, met her glance, and nodded hello with a weak embarrassed smile. Timothy was going to give me gray hair for sure. I waited for the nun to disappear.

OCTOBER: LUNCH WITH JESUS

"You *know* what," I said again through my teeth. "You are not Jesus," I said in a tone that was more like an order than a statement.

"I know," he sighed as I yanked him through the classroom doorway. I closed the door with a thud, grabbed a chair from one of the front desks, and pushed it toward my desk.

"Sit down," I ordered. I plopped myself into my own chair, spread out another napkin, and placed half the sandwich, two apple quarters, and two of the Oreos on it.

"Sit and eat," I said, calming just a little. I nibbled on the sandwich and watched as Timothy took a bite out of one of the Oreos.

In spite of myself, I began to mellow. After the last bite of sandwich my heart rate had returned to normal and I was beginning to find the entire thing kind of funny.

Timothy caught me watching and grinned back at me, his eyes bright blue.

"I know I'm not Him," he said evenly.

"I know you know," I assured.

He looked squarely at me. "But," he began in a tone that told me that he had thought a lot about what he was about to say, "wouldn't it be neat if I were Him?"

This time I looked back at him. The way he said it made me

really consider his words. I smiled. He knew he had my attention. We were connected.

"I mean wouldn't it be neat if instead of just some kid I was really Him and you . . ." he said, getting a little excited, "and *you* were His teacher when he was a little boy?"

I couldn't help but be intrigued at the thought. And I admitted as much.

"Yes, that would be neat," I said.

I watched as he started on the second cookie. He was incredibly beautiful, with blond hair and perfect soft features.

"You know, Timothy," I said. His eyes met mine. "You really aren't just some kid," I told him. "You're a wonderful little boy."

"Thanks." He smiled sheepishly.

"And," I added pausing, "you really are a lot like Him."

His eyes widened. "Really?" he asked, seeming to hold his breath.

"Really," I promised firmly.

Laughing, he jumped up, threw his arms around me, and hugged me tight. I held him laughing, never enjoying a hug more.

OCTOBER: LUNCH WITH JESUS

4

November

We Are Thankful for Each Other

WE ARE THANKFUL FOR EACH OTHER. I wrote the words big and bold on the blackboard. It was the day before Thanksgiving break. We had spent the week prior counting our blessings. The list was now quite long. We had begun with the obvious: home, church, school, and family, and had worked our way to the smaller less obvious things: flowers, trees, sunshine, and even a few beloved goldfish. Some of the list was created by me. Some of it was created by my students. Under protest, I insisted upon adding brothers and sisters to the list. They demanded the addition of Tuesday's Pizza Boat lunch.

Every morning I displayed the theme on the blackboard. We

would read it, discuss it, and then share a story about it. Today we were to celebrate each other.

They giggled happily after reading the message. Playfully, they poked at one another and patted each other's backs as we headed to the back of the classroom to share the story.

"Come up with the rest of us, Daniel," I encouraged as casually as I could, once we were seated. I was in a chair ready to read the story, and the children had gathered in a bunch around my feet. As always, they had scrambled anxiously for the spots closest to me. All but Daniel. He tended to linger outside of the circle. Sometimes, with prodding, he would cautiously enter the group, but most times not. I would try to invite him as matter-of-factly as I could. But no matter how gentle my approach, his face flushed to a brilliant shade of crimson. I didn't want to embarrass him, but I longed for him to join in. I figured the quicker he did, the quicker he would become comfortable and confident. Until recently, the children seemed oblivious to his hesitancy, but lately they were beginning to notice.

They listened as I invited him and watched as he remained motionless, declining my offer.

"It's so nice when all of us are together," I stated cheerily, hoping to motivate him. When he again didn't move, I decided to leave it alone and go on. "Let's get to our story," I said, turning my attention to the book.

NOVEMBER: WE ARE THANKFUL FOR EACH OTHER

I began reading and got through the first page before becoming distracted. Several children sat with their backs turned toward me staring steadily at Daniel, while a few others swung their heads back and forth from me to him, waiting to see if there was going to be another move. And if there was, who was going to make it.

I continued reading, hoping that they would settle, not wanting to acknowledge the situation further. But after reading another page, their fidgeting persisted, and I was just about to give up and admonish them when I spotted Rebecka out of the corner of my eye. She was edging her way backward bit by bit toward Daniel until finally she was sitting beside him. She smiled at him. Although he looked embarrassed, he didn't seem to mind. I continued to read as if I hadn't noticed. Ryan was next. Keeping his eyes on me, he picked his bottom up off the floor and, while balancing on his arms and legs looking much like a spider walking backward, he crawled back to Daniel. Picking up on the trend, each one moved from my side to Daniel's. A couple of them crawled on their bellies as if they were wading through a swamp. I kept reading. Some scooted quickly while others edged like snails. I kept reading. One hopped on his bum, bumping his bottom off the floor like a pogo stick. Samantha, who seemed to understand the idea but not the secretiveness, escaped simply by standing up and walking to her classmate's side.

I kept reading. Finally, I found myself sitting alone in my chair reading aloud with at least fifteen feet separating my students and myself. And there they sat surrounding their friend, who was surprisingly calm and attentive. I continued to read. My next move was obvious.

Being careful not to miss a word, I stood up. And while holding the book in one hand and dragging the chair with the other, I moved to join them. Still reading, I settled back into my newly located seat. Through the corner of my eye, I caught a glimpse of their smiles. Daniel's was the brightest.

As I finished the last page of the book I couldn't help but think that if they learned only this from kindergarten, it would be plenty.

5

December

Hark! Harold the Angel Sings

"This is my life. Not *Miracle on 34th Street*!" she all but screamed at me.

"I understand that," I said as soothingly as I could without sounding condescending. "I didn't say it was."

"I didn't say you said it was," she retorted. Now we were starting to sound like a vaudeville act.

"I just said what's the point of all of this? I mean, I know what you people are trying to pull." I was beginning to get offended.

"No one is trying to pull anything, Mrs. Roma. Especially me. I had nothing to do with this. Sister Helga is in charge of the

Christmas play. She decided who got what part, and she decided Harold would play the young boy Jesus, not me."

"Right," she cut in, "why?"

"Why what?" I asked, exasperated.

"Why out of all of these kids was he picked to be Jesus? He can't sing. He can't dance. He can't memorize lines. Why was he chosen?"

"I don't know," I said, exhausted. I was half tempted to point out that I didn't remember singing and dancing being included in Jesus' talents either, but I didn't want to provoke her further.

"I'll tell you why," she fired at me, obviously not exhausted. "Because they know very well that Harold's father and I are getting a divorce, and this is some nun attempt to get us back together."

"Nun attempt" was a funny choice of words but I resisted a smirk.

"I don't know, maybe it is. But it's not an attempt on my part to do anything," I firmly pointed out.

"They think they'll get us in that church on Christmas Eve with those candles and twinkling lights and some sappy sentimental Christmas play and we'll just somehow get all caught up in the mood and miraculously forget about seven years of misery and fall hopelessly in love again."

DECEMBER: HARK! HAROLD THE ANGEL SINGS

She had just spit on me and her eyes were so wild with anger that I found myself amazed at how wide open they were.

I jerked myself away from staring, realizing that I had let the pause linger too long and it was my turn to talk.

"Well, there's still nothing I can do about it," I said. "Sister Helga is still up in her room. Maybe you could go up and talk to her."

"Fine!" she retorted curtly, snatching the pageant permission slip that had begun this whole tirade off the desk.

Carrying it like a club with which she was planning to whack Sister Helga over the head, she stormed down the hallway. I smiled. Not that I knew for sure, but I wouldn't have been surprised at all if Sister Helga and her fellow Sisters were innocently plotting something. Nothing complicated I was sure. However, it would be just like them to think seven years of "marriage misery" could be fixed by a Christmas Eve pageant. But who could blame them? If a bunch of nuns couldn't believe in the miracle of Christmas, then who could?

A few minutes later, my things gathered and ready to leave for the day, I was caught in my own thoughts. Crossing the doorway I yelped, startled, as I ran smack into Mrs. Roma. Her eyes were wild and wide again. This time I'm pretty sure mine were too. They locked together. We were nose to nose and frozen for a split second; then, coming back to life, she shoved a piece of paper into my chest. Helplessly, I took it as she turned on her heels and huffed away. Looking down, I realized it was the signed pageant permission slip. I didn't breathe until I heard the slam of her car door. And I laughed as I listened to the gray Honda whir out of the parking lot.

"DURING THE NEXT THREE WEEKS," boomed the principal's voice through the public address system, "PAGEANT PRACTICE IS TO TAKE TOP PRIORITY. TEACHERS ARE INSTRUCTED BY THE PRINCIPAL, 'ME' (she always felt the need to identify herself), TO IMMEDIATELY SURRENDER ANY CHILD SISTER HELGA REQUESTS TO THE MUSIC ROOM. NOTHING," continued the instructions, "IS MORE IMPORTANT THAN HONORING OUR SAVIOR JESUS CHRIST THROUGH THIS GLORIOUS PRODUCTION. GOD BLESS YOU SISTER HELGA."

The respectful repetition of "God bless you Sister Helga" murmured through the children as we teachers just shrugged. After having put it that way, who could argue?

During the following weeks I did my part, and most times hand-delivered the two shepherds, a wise man, an angel, and, of course, the young boy Jesus as soon as asked. Most times, I admit to having escorted Harold directly to the music room door, even though he could have gotten there himself. Somehow, I felt better about it. I didn't want to be responsible for allowing the young boy Jesus to wander off to Jerusalem or anything.

Although the location of practice was clear, exactly what was going on in there remained the mystery. Showing her years of experience, Sister Helga promptly taped brown grocery bags to the music room window to discourage gawkers, which all of us desperately wanted to be. Throughout the three weeks, classes were interrupted many times a day with just one- and two-word commands of "Wise Men," "Angels," "Weeping Women," and "Jesus." Full sentences had been eliminated to minimize the interruption. I have to admit Harold bristled and then slunk deeper into his chair as if he'd like to sink down into the linoleum floor each time he was bellowed for. But with a glance from me (sometimes he avoided eye contact as long as possible) he would eventually drag himself from his seat. Hand in hand, we made the long walk to the music room. Sometimes he walked so slowly I thought his feet might be coated with cement. Other times, I had to almost push him through the door. A few times I actually had to wait in line for other teachers who had arrived first to push their tentative students through the door. The buzz of the faculty lunchroom proved fruitless. No one had first-hand knowledge. Nothing had been seen through the brown paper, which, after having been tampered with, had since been doubled.

And we joked that we swore Sister Helga had the room soundproofed especially for the occasion.

Secondary information was no easier to come by. The children were tight lipped and gave up almost nothing when we tried to wheedle out even a morsel of information. Harold supplied absolutely nothing but a few monosyllabic grunts in response to my prodding as we lumbered up the hall. One of the fifth grade teachers was said to have overheard one of her students exasperatingly proclaim that the "kid Jesus stinks" and the "little drummer boy won't stop crying." We laughed, but still had no more information than we'd started with. We would just have to wait for the play.

And after we waited, finally the big night was upon us.

The moon hung high in the clear black sky. A speckle of stars dotted the sky and seemed to shine brighter than on any other night. One star, as if taking cues from Sister Helga herself, seemed to be winking at us as it blinked on and off peeking from behind a purple-gray cloud. At about 7:05, carloads of festive families began dribbling into the church parking lot. By 7:20, they were rushing in, then thumping to a stop in front of the big front steps, hurriedly depositing their loads of high-heeled mothers and aunts, proud uncles, careful-stepping grandmothers and grandfathers, scampering younger brothers and sisters, and nostalgic older siblings. The last one out of the car was always the pageant performer himself who often needed a push to get from the car to the sidewalk. The push usually was delivered by a father who by this time had eyeballed what he feared would be the last spot in the lot and was anxious to claim it for his car.

Climbing the church steps, mothers busily pushed their little stars, who were easily spotted because they were the only ones not smiling, toward the door while yanking rambunctious toddlers out of the newly drifted snow. Like right out of a movie, an ever-so-light snow had begun to fall and glistened as if mixed with glitter. The warmth of the church seemed to greet everyone like a hug. The mothers dashed to what they feared might be the last seats available, dragging little ones with mittened hands and calling to their pageant players to "find Sister Helga."

At precisely 7:29, the last father had trekked from the outskirts of the church property. He stomped his way into the back of the church, shook the snow from his coat like a collie while making a brrrrrrrrrrrr growl that only dads can. Then, yanking his hat off his head awkwardly, he smoothed down less hair than he had five years ago and joined his family already nestled in the pew.

And at exactly 7:30, because punctuality is a virtue, Sister Helga raised the curtain on the St. Joseph's Christmas pageant. Standing stiffly at her post just left of the stage only slightly in view, she lifted not a finger as the most glorious production unfolded like a delicate Christmas lily.

The audience sat with rapt attention as the story of Jesus' birth was told. The adults who had heard it a thousand times listened, soothed by its familiar words, watching the faces of the little ones who were hearing its wonderment for the first time. On cue with Sister Helga, who nodded only slightly, the Angel Gabriel warned us. The star in the east led us. Joseph and Mary despaired and rejoiced. Wise men looked wise. Stable animals nodded respectfully. Delighted angels hovered. A little drummer boy played, crying only a little. The boy Jesus sang; he did stink but no one seemed to mind.

After all had been said and all had been done, not a dry eye remained in the church. As the audience rose to its feet, it showered the performers with nothing short of a thunder of applause. The children laughed, basking in their glory. Families slapped backs. Hugging and chuckling, they reminded each other of this part or that. "How about that little drummer boy?" "Wasn't she just the most beautiful Mary?" "I kept telling myself I wasn't going to cry, now look at me!" As they rushed to collect their children, they offered one more round of respectful applause to Sister Helga, who they knew had pulled off nothing shy of a miracle. After all, these were the same children they often couldn't get to school with two shoes on.

DECEMBER: HARK! HAROLD THE ANGEL SINGS

I watched from the base of the altar as each of my students found their families. I waved and called Christmas greetings as they disappeared into the crowd making its way toward the door.

After pointing out Harold's mother to him, I watched as he scampered over to her. She called Merry Christmas to me, her smile broad. Her eyes were happy and dancing. I called back. Seeing Harold's father join them, I watched as together they spoke to Harold animatedly, obviously gushing over his performance. I smiled as I saw them lean to kiss him and then, to my amazement, they kissed each other.

A cluster of nuns who were huddled together giggling in the corner of the church watched them leave.

6

Snow Angels

They wiggled on the floor around my feet, signaling the end of the lesson. "Now let's remember what we've learned today," I said, vying for one more moment of their attention in hopes of proving to myself that I had indeed gotten their attention at all.

Five-year-olds never cease to amaze me. Each afternoon I teach religion in the back of my classroom; me in a chair and the children around me on the "quiet carpet." They wriggle and wriggle, fidgeting and squirming as I read to them and pray to them. And do anything else I can think of to educate their minds and nourish their souls. At a glance, you would never guess they were even hearing me, let alone comprehending or feeling my objective. But after a few years of doing this, I have finally realized that through an occasional somersault they are hearing, understanding, and even feeling.

"We talked about the different ways to pray," I reminded them. "Who can tell me these ways?" I asked.

"Going to church!" someone shouted.

"Good," I complimented.

"Saying prayers," came another. I nodded.

"Singing hymns."

"Doing good."

"Reading the Bible."

"Very good!" I all but squealed. "And why do we do all of these things?" I asked, my voice rising in anticipation.

If only they could answer this last question, I could stamp myself a success. I would know that I had actually taught them something. My stomach almost hurt with the wait.

"To learn about God," came the reply.

I'd like to say it came from above, but to be completely honest, it came from below, very below. Actually, it came from inside a shirt that the responder had pulled up over his face. I was so relieved to get the answer that I was looking for that I didn't have the heart to scold him.

"Thank you, Brian," I said.

"You're welcome." He was muffled under the shirt. I let myself smile and leaned back in my chair.

"You really were listening." I beamed, satisfied. I sat there basking in what I thought was the end of the lesson.

But God seemed to turn to a precocious brown-haired mop top, gently lay a hand on his head, and whisper "listen" into his ear. The lesson was not over yet.

"I know why we need to learn about God," he offered.

"Tell us," I said, not even giving him my full attention as I began gathering my things.

"So that when we get to Heaven to live with Him we're not strangers." I stopped my gathering.

"Yeah, because that would be so embarrassing," another agreed.

"Yeah, because He knows all about us," someone explained.

The rest nodded in unison. Time stopped for me, but with that they were gone. They went back to their fidgeting, squirming and somersaulting. The shirt over the head fashion had caught on and I had lost many of them to it. I was left alone. I guess the answer, having been obvious to them, didn't merit further contemplation on their part. It was just I who had not entertained this fact, who had to absorb it.

Finally, I smiled and allowed the notion to surround me. I had been pleasantly surprised at receiving the unexpected. I was even a bit embarrassed that they had rewritten my lesson. I wondered where their inspiration had come from. But then casting my eyes heavenward, I think I felt a tap on my own shoulder.

Later that day, as I sat alone in my classroom nibbling on my lunch, I spotted the burgundy leather Bible that sat on the corner of my desk. I cringed a bit, noticing that a thin layer of dust had accumulated on the cover, testifying to my neglect. I was staring at it, motionless, caught in my own thoughts, when a clamor from outside startled me. The children had just been released for recess. I shrugged it off, as this was the ritual every afternoon. I often heard them faintly through the closed window. After another moment, I realized that today it sounded different. It sounded happier. Although the window had been shut tight to the frigid January day, I heard them quite clearly. They certainly were excited. Curiosity getting the best of me, I got up from my seat to see what the extra commotion was all about. Peering out the window, I laughed aloud as I saw every member of my class lying flat on their backs in the snow that had fallen overnight. They were wildly flapping their arms and legs creating snow angel versions of themselves. The nuns who monitored recess scampered, weaving excitedly among them, reprimanding each and ordering them to get up. I laughed louder as I watched them chase each and every one of them back into the building. Once all were inside the door was slammed so loudly I could hear the sound of the clanging metal from where I stood. As the sound of their laughter lingered, then faded away, I stared out of the window at the imprints of snow angels that now dotted the crystal white play yard. Oddly, I counted them. There were twenty-three. Each one had made one. I blinked, stirring myself from my thoughts. I walked from the window and returned to my desk. Plopping myself into my chair, the smile still lingered on my face. Out of the corner of my eye I spotted the Bible again. Grinning heavenward, I whispered, "Okay, okay." And, after wiping my hands, I picked it up gently. Carefully, I caressed it clean. It had been much too long since I had held it, let alone opened it.

"It's all in here," I thought, "everything I need to know about God."

"Yeah, 'cause He knows all about us." The innocent words rang in my ears.

I daydreamed I was at the gates of Heaven, being welcomed into a glorious paradise by God. And I envisioned myself stepping closer to Him as He said, "Welcome, I know all about you." I felt the warmth of His embrace as He hugged me. I heard myself say, "I know all about you too." I picked up the Bible and began to read. I had gotten their attention and they had indeed gotten mine.

7

February

A Cold Chill

My coworker Beth and I stood in the doorway of the classroom watching her walk down the hallway. She wore a plaid green uniform jumper, white kneesocks, and a Barbie backpack strapped to her back. Her navy blue shoes clicked on the linoleum floor as she made her way toward us. Unable to take our eyes off her, we studied her sadly. Although she was no more than forty-five inches tall and about as many pounds, we envisioned her to be supporting the weight of the world on her tiny shoulders.

"Good morning, Samantha," I said as she approached. She glanced up quickly and managed a small "Good morning" in response.

She quickly pushed the white piece of paper that she had been carrying at me and scurried past us and into the classroom. We watched her a moment more as she hurried into the kindergarten to unpack her school bag and hang up her coat. The two of us exchanged worried glances. I looked at the note. I could feel my face tighten and in spite of myself, my eyes filled with tears. I handed it to Beth. She read the words that had been carefully printed on the page. The words that one by one pierced our hearts.

"PLEASE EXCUSE SAMANTHA'S ABSENCE FROM SCHOOL LAST WEEK DUE TO THE DEATH OF HER MOTHER."

I read the signature at the bottom of the note, wondering whose it was. I decided that it was probably a grandmother. My heart ached, imagining what it must have been like to take pen to paper and actually write such a sentence. Fifteen words that cuttingly describe a change in one five-year-old little life.

"What do I do?" I asked Beth pleadingly. Suddenly I felt so overwhelmed. The feeling of wanting to comfort Samantha so badly coupled with my feeling of helplessness panicked me.

"Just be there for her, I guess," she offered. I could tell she was feeling helpless herself. I sighed. Feeling desperately inadequate, I could only hope that somehow what Samantha needed from me would become clear.

"I remember when my grandmother died," I began. My thoughts took me back to an earlier time and it was as if I were thinking out loud. "A very kind man who came to her funeral told me to talk to her. He told me that she could hear me and see me and that she was watching over me. I'm not sure how that sounds but I always remember it. Because it really did help me." Beth nodded. "Maybe that's part of the answer," she offered with a sympathetic nod.

Throughout the day I studied Samantha coming to and from the rest room, on her way back and forth to the office, and in and out of the playground. On the surface she appeared okay, but looking a little closer I saw glimpses of sadness. Sometimes they were as obvious as the way she fidgeted with her hair or the way she bit her lip. Other times they were as subtle as the way she stared out the window or rested her head on her hands. I tried to catch her eye, but she never made eye contact.

I didn't want to fuss over her too much, but I longed to connect with her. Later in the day my class shared recess with Beth's class. Beth and I stood together as the children played before us. Thirty-some children running, jumping, hooting, and hollering. Games of tag, hide-and-seek, and catch clashed together.

"She looks fine," Beth commented, tracking Samantha with her eyes as she weaved in and out of the mob.

"Yes, she does," I agreed, spotting her. I smiled, watching her playfully tease a little boy by wagging her tongue at him. She had her fingers in her ears and she flapped her arms as she wiggled her hips.

"She seems *more* than fine," I laughed. Beth laughed with me. But just as quickly, our laughter disappeared. Because, of course, we both knew that she wasn't fine. Certainly she was far from fine. She had just suffered the greatest loss one can know. There's no greater love than the love of a mother, so when it is lost there is no greater loss.

I could honestly feel an ache in my heart. No one should be without their mother at five years old.

After a pause, Beth asked, "Do you really think that when people die they can see us?" My mind was on the same thought. This was a notion that I wanted to hold on to. It was something that I needed to believe in.

"Yes, I do," I said positively. "I really do. I'm not exactly sure how it works, but I do think they can see us and hear us when we talk to them. I believe they can help us through the day, like angels I guess."

"I think so too," she said. Although we didn't speak the words, I think we both had decided that although Samantha may no longer have a mother here on earth, she did have an angel watching over her from Heaven. An angel that would somehow, some way be there for her. An angel that would somehow, some way guide her. An angel that would somehow, some way dry a tear, blow a kiss, or give a hug. An angel that, although she wasn't fine now, would help her be fine some day.

We stood there side by side with nothing more to say, soaking up the moment as well as the thoughts. The sun gleamed through the branches of the trees, casting patterns of light to dance on top of us. The children darted around us, speckled with images of shadows and light. The wind blew gently, ruffling the trees. The February air was cold and crisp but felt good just the same. We enjoyed the beauty a few moments more, then, checking the time that beckoned us back to the present again, we called the children to gather and head back inside.

As we herded them toward the building, I spotted Samantha a few paces ahead of me. I jogged to catch up to her. Awash with new hope, I came up behind her. Gently touching her shoulders, I gave them a playful squeeze.

"I'm glad you're back," I said, taking her hand and giving it a kiss. We continued to jog toward the building hand in hand. She looked up at me, her face emotionless at first, then suddenly blossoming into a smile. She giggled happily loping beside me.

As we ran enjoying the cold breeze that glided over our faces, I decided that if Samantha's mother was looking down and could see her, then she could see me too. And that being true, I wanted her to know that I was there to help.

CATERPILLAR KISSES

8

March

Marching in the Other Guy's Shoes

Unfortunately, it was quiet when he fell. Actually it wasn't just quiet; it was silent, completely silent. But to be more accurate, he didn't just fall. First he tripped. Then he stumbled. Then he seemed to somehow fly through the air, and then he fell. Not to mention that when he finally did land on the floor, his left shoe shot off. Gawking up from flat on the floor, his face was bright red, his hair disheveled, and his glasses were hanging crookedly across his face.

"Jacob!" I gasped, springing up from my chair to his side.

"Are you okay, honey?" I asked.

He scrambled, embarrassed, trying to get up but even then awkwardly fumbling again.

"It's okay, sweetie," I said, trying to console him, my heart breaking at the embarrassment on his face.

"Just take your time; everyone falls sometimes," I soothed. He nodded, too humiliated to speak. Futilely he tried to straighten his glasses but instead only ended up smashing them into his face. And with the shoe still untied and barely hanging from his foot, he limped back to his desk. I let him go, first because he seemed unhurt and second because I knew that his humiliation would only subside when he was in the safe haven of his seat.

Returning to my own desk, I thought it amazing how children can fall so far, so hard, so dramatically, over nothing but their own two feet. I felt particularly bad for Jacob. He was a big child to begin with, taller and heavier than the rest of his classmates. He seemed not quite comfortable in his body. Almost as if it wasn't his own, but instead on loan for the day. And he was trying to get used to it. He reminded me of a bear cub waiting to grow into his oversized paws.

Once seated, I checked on him. He kept his head down, not daring to look up. He fiddled with the objects on his desk and pretended to be busy. His face was now a paler shade of red.

A giggle from two girls huddled together in the first row drew my attention. They whispered around cupped hands as they peeked over their shoulders at him. Without lifting his head, Jacob raised his eyes to see them. His face reddened again.

"Let's get back to work," I directed sternly.

They hushed. I surveyed the class. All heads were down and busy now. Jacob's head hung a little lower. My heart ached for him. I tried to concentrate on my own work. A moment later a giggle called me. Then another. Then another.

"Let's get back to work," I ordered, my voice possessing an edge that I disliked. I watched Jacob sink deeper into his chair.

This time the silence lasted only a moment. Then more giggles peppered the classroom. I took a deep breath.

"Jacob," I called. His head shot up. "Can you please take this to the office for me?" I asked, holding out a large yellow envelope.

He sat motionless. I was sure the prospect of leaving his seat again petrified him. But I felt I needed to speak to the others. He looked me square in the face as if begging me to read his mind and reconsider. But when I didn't, he gulped hard as I held the envelope toward him. I nodded encouragingly. Hesitantly he rose, then, gingerly stepping toward me, he walked as if the tiles on the floor were numbered and he was trying to manipulate them in sequence. Finally, he reached me, took the envelope, and left the room.

I faced my students. Silently, they looked back at me. They

knew what was coming. Some of them refused to make eye contact.

"I'm disappointed," I said. Their eyes widened at such a harsh statement and they dropped their heads in shame.

"You need to be better friends to each other than that," I reminded.

"When something happens to someone else, when someone has an embarrassing moment, you need to put yourself in their shoes, and think of how you would like to be treated. Then treat them the same way."

I shook my head sternly at them. I could tell they understood. But just for good measure, I spoke squarely to the two girls in the front row who had started all of the giggling. "Put yourself in the other guy's shoes," I repeated.

They hung their heads. I returned to my desk.

In a moment, Jacob appeared back in the doorway. He stopped. Eyeing the distance between the doorway and his desk with trepidation, he sighed loudly and with a burst of gumption, he marched to his seat. His classmates peeked up from their work ever so carefully. Some of the more sympathetic ones looked just as relieved as Jacob that he arrived safely.

A few minutes later they were lined up at the door ready for recess. Before I dismissed them, I looked at them sternly one last time. "Think about my words," I reminded.

CATERPILLAR KISSES

A short thirty minutes later, we were together again in the classroom, them at their seats, me at my desk. Our heads were bowed and our hands were folded. We were ready to begin our afternoon as we always did, with a prayer.

"Thank you God for this day," I began like I always did.

"Thank you for all that we are learning today. Help us to grow in love and faith." Raising my head just slightly, I checked on them. All heads were bowed. All hands were folded.

I was just about to reclose my eyes when I glanced down and noticed it. At first, I was sure that I was mistaken. "I must not be seeing what I think I'm seeing," I thought to myself. But after a longer look, I found that I wasn't mistaken. They had remembered my words, all right. They had just remembered different ones than I had expected.

"Thank you for keeping us safe," I said as I rose from my seat, my voice rising as well. I walked among them. A few at a time noticed that I noticed and began squirming uncomfortably in their chairs. Some of them squeezed their eyes closed tighter and folded their hands so tightly their knuckles were white.

"Thank you for all of the many gifts you shower upon us and please help us to be deserving of them," I said, speaking even louder just to watch them fidget more. "But most of all, God," I emoted, pausing for dramatic effect, "please, please, please," I lamented, "let us put our own shoes on our own feet before beginning our afternoon lessons." I drew my breath as if to indicate that there might be more. They froze, but I simply said, "Amen."

Too frightened to move, their eyes were glued to me. "Amen," I reminded them in a whisper that shook them out of their shock.

"Amen," they whispered back at me. I fought to keep the smile off my face.

"I'll just give you all a minute," I told them gently, then turned my back to them.

They sprang into action behind me. It started slowly and then quickly rolled over the classroom like a wave as they dropped to the floor feverishly trying to put themselves back into their own shoes and out of the other guy's.

When I finally trusted myself to face them without laughing, I turned to find a very confused Jacob standing among the flurry of activity.

Looking puzzled, he stared down at his own shoes, but after a few moments of study, finding nothing amiss, he passed it off with a shrug and walked to his seat.

9

April

April Showers

The harsh April rain beat against the classroom windowpanes. I sat at my desk reading my daily Bible passage as my students sat at their desks reading books of their own choosing. During these twenty minutes of each day, the entire school enjoyed a time of silent reading. It was an effort to break away from the rigors of organized academics and read for enjoyment. Most days it seemed to work, and I would find my students glued to the pages of their books. Those who were able to read did, and those who were not yet able to read scrutinized the pictures.

But today the children were distracted by the rain. It was quite a storm. The sky had darkened to an ominous black so much that, even with the bright overhead lighting, the classroom had a smoky, almost spooky aura about it. The wind gushed and the drops pelted the windows even harder. The children shifted uncomfortably in their seats. It was at times like this that they showed their age. Their wide eyes testified they were only five.

"It's only rain," I reminded them. "Try to keep reading."

The storm was so fierce that it seemed as if someone was throwing pails of water at the windows. For a few moments it slowed, and we were lulled back into a bit of security. We read again. Then, without warning, thunder exploded and sent a shower of hail shooting against the windows. Many of my students yelped, startled, while others gasped then held their breath, all of their frightened eyes darting nervously from the window to me. I admit to having been startled myself.

"Wow! That was a big one!" I acknowledged cheerily, willing my voice to sound normal.

But before my tone could take effect, the thunder rumbled again. The children grimaced and many of them slunk down in their chairs. I closed my book. A few of them had their eyes glued on me and were so frightened that they mimicked my actions and slammed their own books shut and waited for instructions. They seemed to be anticipating that I might scream, "Head for the hills!" and run toward the door. They sat on the edges of their chairs. I smiled reassuringly.

"I know it seems like more. But really, it's only rain. You're perfectly safe. I'm sure of it."

A few of them smiled back. A hand flew into the air.

"Yes?" I called.

"My mom says the rain is God crying," she offered.

"My mom says it's Jesus crying."

"My mom says it's the angels crying."

"Well, my Gram says it's got *nothing* to do with anybody at all crying," Emma emphatically stated. "The rain is God's way of washing us all clean. 'Cause we're all dirty of sin."

"I'm not dirty of sin," an offended David blurted, taking exception.

"We're ALL dirty from sin," Elizabeth insisted sternly. "The Bible says so."

He shot her an angry look but chose not to compete with the Bible. The boys in the class learned early that a scripture-spouting female was someone to be reckoned with.

Catherine nodded in my direction. "Isn't that right, teacher?"

"Well," I murmured slowly, buying myself some time.

Without warning, I had been tossed square into a field of land mines and was anxious to tiptoe my way out.

APRIL: APRIL SHOWERS

"I have to say that I really don't know if the rain is anyone at all crying," I began, trying to stay as neutral as possible.

"But I do like the idea of washing us clean. That kind of sounds nice," I offered.

"But are we all dirty from sin?" David pressed.

"The Bible *says* so," Cara insisted, annoyed that this point was still in question.

I was beginning to wonder why, out of all the Bible passages I've read them, they all seemed to remember that one.

"Well," I mused again, "I think we all have a tiny bit of sin that could use washing away. But I really don't think any of you are sinful."

This seemed to somewhat satisfy them and I was relieved that no hands were raised. The rain seemed to be easing up as well, so I shooed them back to their books. But barely into the first paragraph, a clap of thunder rocked the classroom and we were back where we started.

"Teacher," Eric began nervously, "what if God is mad at us 'cause of all of our sin?"

"Yeah," Joshua piped up, eyeing the storm warily.

"He's not mad at us," I assured them.

"He could be," Daniel protested. "Sometimes I'm kinda bad."

"I lied once," Jason croaked.

"I took my sister's gum," Erin confessed.

CATERPILLAR KISSES

I was unable to stop the flood of confessions that poured out of them as the rain poured down the windowpanes. When they were finished, I tried to console them.

"I understand that you've all done things that you shouldn't have," I began, "but I can see that you're all very sorry for them. And God can see that too. So I know He forgives you. I'm sure He's not mad."

They didn't believe me. It was obvious from their faces. I went back to my book. I tried to ignore them but with the weight of their eyes upon me, it wasn't easy. I stared at the page pretending to read. They didn't even pretend; they just stared at me. The wind howled and again the thunder crashed. Their eyes darted from me to the window. A few hands flew into the air, but refusing to look up, I acted as if they weren't there. Then bravely someone spoke.

"Teacher, He sounds pretty mad." I looked up to find the rest of their heads bobbing in agreement. They were completely serious. It touched and amused me. I closed my book.

"I'm really very sure God's not mad," I repeated softly. "Certainly not at us anyway. I just think it's a storm."

"But maybe He's waiting for us to get washed clean."

I could see where this was headed and instantly began shaking my head back and forth.

"We are not going out there," I stated firmly.

Now please let me explain how we ended up out there. I really hadn't intended on letting them run through a thunderstorm. It's just that they called my bluff. After way too much conversation that circled and went nowhere, I found them completely unconvinced that God wasn't waiting for them to wash themselves clean. And no matter how hard I tried to convince them otherwise, they persisted. Finally I agreed that, if it would put them at ease, we would go out to the courtyard windows and take a peek. I really thought we were just going to take a peek. I was sure that by the time we got down there either the rain would have stopped or at least slowed enough for me to say, "See, God obviously wasn't mad. He had just been giving the grass a good long drink." Or if the rain hadn't stopped, they would surely chicken out once down there. As it turns out neither happened.

Having no business at all being out of our classroom, we crept down the hallways like a pack of thieves, ducking as we passed doorways. We took the long way around the inside of the building, avoiding the school's office. The children shushed each other and crept down the stairwell to the basement.

Once at the bottom, they huddled shoulder to shoulder at the window with their noses pressed against the glass. I found the light switch and flipped it on. The bulb burst on with an abnormally bright light, made a crackling sound, flickered, and went out. I rolled my eyes. I just couldn't get a break. A few of them noticed and eyed me warily.

"It's nothing," I barked.

The others were too distracted to notice and continued to regard the storm with amazement. There was just enough light seeping through the windows to cast a glimmer of light upon them. I was taken by their profiles; they literally glowed.

"Well, who's going first?" I challenged, half mocking but completely sure I would have no takers.

Then to my amazement a hand rose tentatively in the back. I craned my neck to see who it was attached to.

"Eric?" I questioned.

"Yeah," he nodded.

I felt bad that he viewed punching his brother quite so seriously. I almost felt obligated to tell him that if half of what the fourth grade teacher says about his brother was true, then he probably deserved a good punching anyway.

He stepped forward like a brave, yet frightened warrior.

"I really don't think He's waiting for us to wash ourselves clean," I stated again.

Their minds remained unchanged.

"Just in case," someone offered from the back.

Eric edged closer to my shoes.

"Okay," I sighed, giving up. "You want to go out there?" I asked looking square into his eyes. He nodded.

"Just for a minute," I warned, not believing I had gotten myself trapped into this.

It was still pouring outside. I pushed hard on the heavy metal door but had to try a second time, throwing my hip into it to get it to budge. Once the door was open, Eric paused on the threshold letting the rain splatter his face. Then like a skydiver he jumped out into the rain. He stood completely still in the middle of the courtyard for a moment, then slowly turned to face me. I nodded, and he darted back inside. I laughed as he collapsed onto the linoleum floor. He smiled through rain-drenched eyelashes.

"You must be clean," I exclaimed. "Because you certainly are wet. Do you feel better?" I asked.

He nodded, giggling.

"Anybody else?" I challenged. Seeing he had come back unscathed, volunteering hands shot into the air. I groaned playfully at them. "You guys are going to get me fired." They laughed, knowing I was kidding.

"Get out there," I ordered playfully to Samantha. She wasted no time crashing through the doorway. She jumped into the courtyard, stretched her arms out to her sides, and spun in circles. I smiled watching her. The rain had intensified, but we hardly noticed. Somehow, it seemed friendlier.

One by one, each of them took a turn washing themselves clean in God's own rain. I was intrigued to find their styles strikingly similar to their personalities. Some charged out the door while others dipped out a toe at a time like testing the temperature of pool water. Once out there, my more flamboyant students danced and stomped while the more timid ones tiptoed and stood perfectly still like embarrassed, soaking wet puppies. Some scrubbed their arms and legs as if they were standing under a shower, while others opened their mouths to let the water rush in. After each had had a turn, I slammed the door shut and looked at them. Their faces beamed with pride. They could not have been more pleased with themselves. They were soaked to the skin. Their clothes wrinkled around them and their hair matted to their heads. They looked adorable.

"Satisfied?" I laughed, already knowing the answer. They nodded yes and giggled naughtily.

"We better get back upstairs," I said and took a step toward the stairs. A voice squeaked from the back.

"What about you, teacher?" it questioned. "Don't you have any sin that needs washing clean?"

"Boy do I," I thought to myself.

"Yeah, maybe you have just a tiny bit of sin to wash off too?" George suggested gently. He was always a diplomat and careful not to accuse. I appreciated his tact.

APRIL: APRIL SHOWERS

67

Their eyes searched me, waiting for my reply.

"I think I do." I smiled, not really believing I was actually going to do this. I chuckled as I forced the metal door open. I took a deep breath and crossed over to the other side. I heard them scrambling behind me for vantage points along the windowsills. Trying a few of the techniques they had modeled for me, I raised my arms into the air and let the drops splash me in the face. Just for good measure I turned around just once. I laughed in spite of myself and when I turned to face them, their smiles were bright through the glass. I was just about to attempt another spin when I was stopped suddenly, catching a glimpse of Ronald's face dropping into wide-eyed fear. Puzzled, I looked at him. He was looking beyond me up to the second floor windows above us. I followed his gaze to see what he saw. And what he saw nearly stopped my heart: the black silhouette of a crossed-armed nun staring down on me alone in the courtyard. I all but yelled "yikes," pulled my arms in, closed my mouth, and scurried to the door. Their faces were pressed to the window, all of them serious now having seen what Ronald saw. I yanked the door open, somehow easily now, this fear giving me the strength of Atlas. I jumped through the doorway and slammed it shut. I darted to the head of the line and began charging up the stairs taking them two at a time. Without need for instruction they formed a line and scrambled behind me. Much quicker than we had crept down, we stole our way through the corridors and back toward the classroom. The squeaks and squeals of our wet shoes and clothes drew some attention from the classrooms we passed but we were out of sight so quickly that no one really paid much mind.

Finally, a few frantic moments later we had reached the haven of our room. They sat straight backed and scared to death in their chairs. I flopped into my seat. Their eyes were wide on me.

"You guys are going to get me fired," I exclaimed in little more than a whisper. This time they weren't sure I was kidding, and neither was I.

I sighed, letting the breath I had been holding rush out. But as scared as I was I was still unable to keep a smile from appearing on my face. If the truth were told, I hadn't done anything that fun in a long time. All of a sudden, they were smiling back at me. But just as quickly my smile disappeared again as a sound from the hallway drew my attention. Wanting to be sure, I pressed a finger to my lips asking them for silence. They hushed. I became sure of the sound.

"Try to look dry," I ordered, rolling my eyes, knowing full well just how impossible that was.

"And read," I added, nodding to the books that were still on their desks. Feebly they straightened their clothes and pressed their hair. They stared unblinkingly at the books.

I grabbed my own book and waited for the sound to get

closer. The squeaking of rubber-soled shoes creeping along the wet linoleum grew louder. Finally, Sister Marie presented herself in the doorway. Frowning, she surveyed the children. They were perfectly still; not one head rose. She furrowed her brow, then cast her eyes on me. She waited and, when I offered nothing, she raised her eyebrows in question. I offered her only the faintest smile, pleading with her to trust me maybe just this once.

"Everything okay in here?" she asked.

"Just fine, Sister," I answered, probably too quickly.

She stared at me a moment longer as if to say that if she really wanted to find out what was going on in here she could. Then, looking over the children again, she seemed to flinch noticing their wet heads. They hadn't moved. She frowned again as she looked back at me. But I could tell she wasn't all that mad. Then looking out the window, she offered with a nod, "The storm's over."

She said it with a tone that suggested that she had seen quite a few storms in her seventy years. The children's heads shot toward the window, their eyes wide as they stared.

"The sun's coming out," she added as she turned and crept out of the doorway. I was grateful she didn't come back when she heard their cheers of joy.

10

May

The Field Trip

He stood cross armed and serious as his father read the poster tacked to the wall. I watched them curiously from inside the classroom. I was seated at my desk, preparing the day's lessons. Even though they were about twenty feet away, I could see and hear them clearly. The frown on the father's face was obvious, as was the determination on the boy's.

"You're supposed to use that one," the boy ordered, pointing impatiently to the pen dangling from a string that I had taped to the wall. The father shot him a look as if he might snap at him, but instead he huffed and pushed his own pen back into his shirt pocket and grabbed the one that was hanging there in mid-swing. He pulled it too far, but it held firm and yanked him back.

"That's so you can't steal it," pointed out the son. I muffled a laugh as the father assured him through gritted teeth that he had no intention of stealing the pen. He gave a low growl and shifted closer to the wall. He crouched and penned his name on the third line.

"Good," answered the son cheerily. Then using traditional teacher logic that I had obviously used more than I thought I had, he took the present situation and generalized it, then wrapped it up and handed it back to his father. "Because if everyone came here and stole pens, what kind of place would this be?" he asked. The look on his face seemed to commend his father for his high moral choice against theft.

The father looked squarely at him and, for a second, the way he twisted his lips, it looked again as if he might say something back. But, probably thinking what in the world was he going to say to a five-year-old who was asking a rhetorical question, he stayed silent.

The bell rang, ending the stalemate.

"You better get in there," the father said as pleasantly as anyone could who was as annoyed as he was. "School's starting."

"I know. That's what the bell is for," the boy explained.

I stifled a chuckle. Talk about being saved by the bell. These two needed saving from each other.

"Carl," I called, beckoning him in. He smiled at me and darted into the room.

I waved and called a small good morning to Mr. Edwards. Confused at first, he looked behind himself to see who I was waving at. Realizing it was him that I was waving at, he offered a gesture that was more like swatting me away than it was waving to me. He muttered, "Yeah." I guessed that was his version of hello. He turned and disappeared out of the doorway. I smiled and thought, God bless anyone who gets in his way today.

Carl hurriedly hung his sweatshirt and unpacked his school bag. As he stuffed his belongings into his desk, still standing, he waved his hand frantically in the air trying to get my attention.

"Yes, Carl?"

"My dad's coming on the field trip to the zoo," he announced.

"He is?" I said, trying to act surprised as well as excited. "That's great."

"Yep. He just signed the list today," he said, motioning toward the hall. "He doesn't want to go though. My mom's making him. She says if he doesn't start getting interested in me, I'm gonna get wrecked and grow up rotten and be a big disaster when I'm old—like twenty." He added this last part thoughtfully, nodding his head sadly as if he had just heard a horrible story about some poor kid gone bad. This time I didn't bother to hide it and just laughed heartily.

"Well, none of us wants to see you grow up wrecked," I assured him.

"Thanks," he nodded gratefully, "especially my mom," he added. "She says over her dead body."

"Well, let's hope it won't come to that," I said.

The day of the field trip arrived, and so did Carl's father, and so did Carl's father's cell phone. It was plastered to his ear as he stood in the hallway waiting for the field trip bus to arrive. He stood in the middle of the corridor bent at the waist, with the index finger of the hand that was not holding the phone plugged into his ear. He stood surrounded by the group of children who had been assigned to him. He dodged, ducked, twisted, and turned trying futilely to escape the noise. He looked as if he were stomping on ants. If it wasn't so funny, I probably would have felt sorry for him. But so far, he was kind of hard to feel sorry for. The conversation he was attempting to have obviously wasn't going well because he kept repeating himself and screaming into the phone. I entertained the thought of trying to help him out a bit by shushing the children, but from experience I knew that trying to silence twenty-five field trip–bound five-year-olds never worked anyway. Instead, I walked by, slapped a name tag on him, and ruffled Carl's hair.

"I'm really glad your dad decided to come," I whispered with a wink.

"Me too," he said with a smile broader than I had ever seen on him. He grabbed his father's hand that had temporarily become unplugged and cupped it between the two of his. Annoyed, his father shook it free and peered down disgustedly at the name tag. He rolled his eyes as he read his printed name. I stopped and frowned not so much in my defense, but in Carl's. Embarrassed that he had been caught, awkwardly the father tried to stroke Carl's hair. But Carl, who had obviously been shook off before and who seemed oblivious to the fact that his feelings should have been hurt, pretended that his father's hand, which was now resting on his head, was crushing him. He made a groaning sound, stuck his tongue out of the side of his mouth, closed his eyes, and collapsed to the floor. His classmates squealed hysterically.

Realizing that he was fighting a battle he could not win, Mr. Edwards let out a groan of his own, then yelled into the phone, "I'll call you back." He yelled this much too loudly. It startled the children and they became instantly silent. They stared wide-eyed at him waiting for more. But when they realized there was not going to be any more, they recovered from his outburst, collectively found this outrageously funny, and dissolved into laughter again. Mr. Edwards sighed, made a face as if he had a bad taste in his mouth, and stood perfectly still and slightly slumped over. He looked defeated.

The screech of the metal brakes from the school bus pulling up to the curb drew our attention.

"Let's go!" I called. Their shouts of joy were deafening.

After much scrambling and negotiating with promises to "be your best friend until I die" or to "give you my lunch dessert for a week," everyone was finally planted in a seat that satisfied them. Ready to pull out of the parking lot, I walked the aisle of the bus, gently touching mops of hair as I counted them.

"Twenty-five?" I announced with a question in my voice. "Someone's missing," I called, feigning confusion. Then, as if startled by a brainstorm, I tapped my own head and yelled, "Twenty-six. That's better!" In adult circles, I am not considered humorous. Among kindergartners I'm a riot. They were hysterical.

I raised my voice and began a prayer. They settled and joined me, bowing their heads. The bus engine coughed, then roared strong. We continued our prayer as the bus slowly whirred out of the parking lot. "Amen," we finished in unison.

I raised my head to find Mr. Edwards's motionless body standing in the center of the aisle. He was bent at the waist and was staring out the window with a horrified look on his face. He was staring at the school's secretary who was standing on the sidewalk waving his cell phone at the bus, which was now gaining speed out of the parking lot. He had apparently set the phone down during one of the many times he stopped to dust off his pants after one of the children brushed up against him. It was hard to imagine him of all people forgetting his phone but I guess the distraction of the children can get to just about anyone, even the most disinterested. I watched the secretary until she was merely a dot on the sidewalk. I've never seen a more heartbroken man.

"Don't worry," was all I could offer. "She'll take good care of it," I said, turning to hide the smile that was threatening to overtake my face. I settled into my own seat and tried to stifle a laugh. Behind me I could hear him growl as he settled into his seat.

Thirty minutes later we arrived at the zoo. After quickly breaking into groups, we rushed through the zoo gates like a SWAT team taking siege. The children danced around their assigned chaperones as the adults moseyed from area to area. The grown-ups encouraged the children to slow just a bit to enjoy and take in each exhibit. But the children just begged the adults to hurry and get to the next gate. By the fourth or fifth display, we seemed to somehow reach a compromise, falling into a rhythm that satisfied everyone. We began to relax and enjoy the zoo that sat picture perfect beneath the clearest bluest sky and sparkling yellow sun. We all seemed to relax. All of us, that is, except

MAY: THE FIELD TRIP

Mr. Edwards. Somehow you could not use the word "relaxed" to describe him. "Resigned" might be more suitable. He seemed resigned to his fate. Miserably resigned, to be specific. I couldn't tell if it was the longing he felt for his cell phone or the raw deal he felt he had gotten for being with us in the first place, but he had a miserable look on his face. He kept his jaw so taut that the muscles in the sides of his face were pulsating. The good news is Carl seemed unaware of his father's mood and joined his classmates as they danced around Mr. Edwards's legs, circling his waist. Seeming completely unaccustomed to caring for children, Mr. Edwards made awkward attempts to direct them forward and corral them, but he either stumbled over them or they tripped over him. Finally, he settled for a place slightly behind them, sporadically counting them, pointing his finger with his hand still discreetly down at his side.

Actually, he was doing a pretty good job. Only once did I find him confused. Counting to three he stalled, furrowed his brow, and asked the lady next to him, "Is the kid in the red mine or yours?" Proud of being an experienced chaperone she curtly said, "Yours," and turned on her heel. Noting her tone, Mr. Edwards rolled his eyes, then scanned the crowd for his two other charges.

About a quarter of the way through the zoo, we found ourselves huddled at everyone's favorite display, the elephants. Part of the class was already there. Shortly, the rest of us joined them. The children stood perched with their feet on the bottom rung of the fence. The adults stood behind them enjoying the lull from the maddening pace. Together, we marveled at the elephants' size. No matter how old you are or how many times you have seen them, it's still a marvel. The children stood mesmerized, gawking through wide eyes. And the adults seemed to enjoy that there still were a few things left in this world that intrigued them.

For several minutes, we gazed lazily as a single elephant lumbered slowly around the area. He wasn't doing much, but the movement alone was fascinating. I glanced along the top rail of the fence, enjoying the profiles of twenty wondering five-year-olds. From each experience, I like to capture a picture in my head to save for later. From this trip, this would be the picture. The moment lasted only a second.

"Hey!" someone called from the middle of the line. "Here comes another one!"

The garage door–like gates on the building behind the display creaked open and another elephant stepped out into the sunlight. He moved slowly as if he had just been awakened from a deep sleep. The children squealed and chattered excitedly. And, as if to express his excitement as well, the elephant raised his trunk and spoke back to us, trumpeting loudly. I couldn't have planned it better. The children were thrilled. Some of them waved and called to him; others bellowed back, lifting their own arms in a trunklike fashion.

"Look! He's gonna do another trick," someone noted. The children directed their attention as the elephant curiously seemed to march in place, high stepping his huge loglike legs. It seemed odd that they could bend at the knee. We were perfectly silent as he held our rapt attention. He marched for another second or two, then strangely began turning in circles. Without a sound or a clue, we continued to watch. Mr. Edwards, the only one with a bit of a clue, muttered ever so softly so that only I could hear, "It ain't gonna be a trick."

I turned back to him, frowning. I didn't want him to ruin the moment. But here we seemed to be in a different moment than I thought we were. I turned around just in time to watch the largest load of poop fall out of the behind of our elephant friend and plop onto the ground. We were awestruck. No one moved. It didn't even seem like anyone was breathing. With our mouths hanging open, no one knew what to say. Then from behind us, to knock us back to life, came a voice. It was Mr. Edwards' voice. He said, "It was a poop trick." He stood casually propped against the fence behind us nodding his head knowingly.

It was all the children needed to bring them to life. In a frenzy they broke into hysterical shrieks of laughter, holding their noses, clutching their stomachs, covering their eyes. Collectively they repeated, "It was a poop trick." This was absolutely the funniest thing they had ever heard.

Mr. Edwards, still leaning against the fence, looked at them, puzzled, as if he had never been funny before and certainly hadn't intended on being funny this time either. But like it or not, he had been funny. More than funny, he had been hysterical. And what's more, he had just become our class hero. So much so that by the time we were able to reluctantly drag the children away from the elephant exhibit, he was surrounded by children. Like the Pied Piper, he led them through the rest of the zoo. The children squirmed to get spots closest to him. Those who couldn't get close enough to grab hold of one of his fingers settled for a snag of clothing. The rest of the remaining mother chaperones and I walked behind. But to tell the truth we were unneeded. He could have easily done it all himself.

Mr. Edwards and his adoring fans strolled through the zoo, every once in a while breaking into spontaneous chants of, "It's a poop trick," then dissolving into squeals of laughter.

Mr. Edwards was a changed man. His hearty chuckles could easily be heard above the rest. He was at ease with his newfound celebrity and chatted comfortably with the children. Although what he said seemed to make little or no sense, they somehow understood him perfectly. And what his observations lacked in educational value they made up for in hilarity. Actually, the students found everything he said funny whether he meant it to be or not.

By the time we boarded the bus headed back to school, most of the children were exhausted from laughing. One particularly disgruntled mother asked me if I intended to put a stop to it. But since I had no such intention, I just pretended not to hear her. Frankly, I thought it was wonderful. I had enjoyed watching the transformation of this man. And I especially enjoyed seeing the beaming pride on Carl's face. After all, this hero was his dad. I could tell you that it ended there, but actually, it had just begun. The ensuing thirty-minute bus ride back was by far the fullest bus ride I had ever experienced.

Mr. Edwards took over completely. All I had to do was sit back and enjoy. He began with jokes.

"Why did the poop cross the road? To get to the other side of course."

"Knock knock?"

"Who's there?"

"Poop!"

"Poop who?" No punch line was ever needed for this one. By the third line they were all laughing so loudly no one would have heard it anyway.

Next he moved on to an endless array of smoosh faces which

he achieved by using his hands to push, pull, and stretch his face into a variety of contortions. They all looked the same to me, but apparently there were differences that were visible, and hysterical, only to the children.

After that, he entertained them with interesting sounds. One of the sounds he made by popping his finger out of the side of his air-filled cheek. Another he made by tapping on his pushed-out stomach. And the last one, which I could have done without, he made with his armpit.

By the time we were pulling into the school's parking lot he was frantically leading the children through the last few choruses of "Ninety-nine Bottles of Holy Water on the Wall."

Once back in the classroom, I could barely get the children to let go of him. Finally, I was able to convince them to return to their seats by insisting that he would only be able to sign the chaperone list for the next field trip if they would let go. With big bold strokes, he signed the list. They cheered.

"Carl, can you say good-bye to your dad in the hall?" I asked.

Proudly, Carl escorted the hero to the door. I spied them from my seat. Once again, I could see and hear them clearly. They looked at each other with silent satisfied grins.

"You're a great dad," Carl said.

Taken aback, Mr. Edwards hesitated, then swallowing he said, "You're a great kid."

MAY: THE FIELD TRIP

Carl nodded and smiled.

"See you tonight," said the father.

"See you tonight," said the son.

We all lined up at the window and waved as his car left the parking lot. He blew his horn the whole way.

11

Caterpillar Kisses

It was the last day of school. As was my habit, I made it a point to arrive early to spend a few moments alone in the classroom. I meandered between the five rows of desks. 5 × 5 = 25. A perfect classroom: just the way I liked it.

Gently, I tapped each name tag as I happened upon it. Once, the tags had been laminated flat and clean to the desk. But in June they showed the ten months of wear they had narrowly survived. Now they were frayed and curling at the edges. They seemed to be wilting under the hot humid air that hovered in the classroom.

When the school year began, they were nothing more than

names printed on cardboard. But here at the end of the year, each was a child, a living, breathing, learning, and laughing child. A child who one day in September was a name that I simply copied from a roster was now, in June, a person I loved.

Reading each name unlocked a glimmer of memory that floated and danced around me. A unique moment, incident, or word that forever marked that child as one of mine. A memory that left a kiss upon my heart that I prayed would stay forever.

Pausing at each desk, I allowed myself to relive a moment that made that child special. As I did, I dropped a photograph on top of the desk that I had taken on the first day of school. I heard my own warning words.

"On the last day of school I will show you this picture again. You won't believe how you will grow." I remember they doubted me.

My heart swelled, looking at each photo. Babies no more.

With the last picture placed, I went to my own desk and retrieved the very last worksheet from our religion book. I removed the paper clip and went to the doorway to wait for them.

Predictably, at exactly 8:23 A.M., I heard the faint roar of the school bus struggling to climb the steep city street to our school. The roar grew louder, and then was silenced by the harsh squeal of the metal brakes. I lingered in the lull of quiet that followed. I could almost see them jumping off the bus, charging across the parking lot passing the morning greeter, aka Sister Regina, who didn't greet them at all but instead shushed them and begged them to slow. They whizzed by her, respectful of her request, but unable all the same to slow the excited little legs that were diving them into their very last day of kindergarten.

I heard the squeak of the front door that had been begging to be oiled since the first day of school, and the charge of youthful feet that quickened into a stampede.

Exactly thirty seconds later they rounded the corner at the end of the hallway and charged toward me. On another day I would have ordered them to slow, but today, I enjoyed the sight of them running right at me.

"Good morning!" I called as they rushed passed me to the promised and much anticipated treasure that lay upon their desks. Each child rushed to their own seat, snatched the photograph of themselves, and then dissolved into a clamor of embarrassed laughs and giggles. At first they clutched the pictures to their chests, feigning modesty. Then, after quick negotiations that included "I'll show you mine if you show me yours," and "I won't laugh if you won't laugh," they exchanged photos and, keeping only half the bargain, squealed to hysteria.

"Have you grown?" I called over the noise. Collectively they turned to me shouting a joyful "Yes!"

"Yes, you have." I laughed.

JUNE: CATERPILLAR KISSES

Later I settled them into the last lesson of the school year.

"This year," I began in a quiet soothing voice, "you have become two things." I held up one finger. "One is a first grader." Their eyes glowed with pride at being called this.

"Does anyone know the other?" Their heads darted around. No hands were raised.

"You have become this," I announced as I turned the worksheet toward them. A pause ensued as they sounded out the words testifying to 180 days of phonics lessons. The hand of my quickest reader darted to the air.

"T.J.?" I nodded.

"A friend of Jesus," he proudly read.

"Yes!" I applauded. "This year you have all become friends of Jesus!"

"You did this," I explained, "because you have spent the year learning about Him. You have prayed to Him, sung about Him, read about Him, written about Him, you have read His book," I reminded them, picking up a Bible, "and you have even visited Him in His house," I said pointing out the window to the church. "He knows all about you. This year, you began learning about Him."

Their smiles broadened.

I passed the papers quickly as they scrambled, reaching for

scissors and crayons. The assignment was to color and cut a button out of paper.

Once they were finished, I pinned the paper buttons to their shirts. I laughed out loud as I watched them puff out their chests in pride.

"What about you, teacher?" someone inquired. "You're Jesus' friend too."

"I am, thank you. I better get busy," I said and quickly cut and colored my own button as the children looked on.

Just as I was about to pin it on, Ronald rushed to my side. "I'll help you!" he insisted, carefully taking the pin and button from me. The rest scurried for a better vantage point. It took his pudgy fingers a while to manipulate the clasp. But before long I, too, was labeled a "Friend of Jesus." I liked the feeling.

"We should wear these out in the hall so that everyone can see us," someone suggested. Heads bobbing in agreement looked to me. It was a good idea.

So, being as quiet as mice, because that is the rule, we walked through the halls of the school joyfully yet silently proclaiming our friendship. Our smiles had never been so proud or so wide. The adults and the older children who already knew how to read greeted us politely. The teachers of the younger ones explained in a whisper what we were up to. All the while my children basked in the attention, enjoying the immense feeling of importance that the message on the button provided.

That afternoon, with their buttons still on, I dismissed them from the front porch of the school for the last time. A lump formed in my throat as I sent them down the steps one at a time to their waiting parents.

Many of the adults squinted trying to read the words on the button. Then as the child drew closer and the words became clear they smiled and nodded in agreement. Many called and waved to me after reading the message.

"You too!" one mother called, pointing to the button pinned to my own shirt.

"You bet," I called back.

Having bid the last of them good-bye, I lingered on the porch a few moments longer. Caught in my own thoughts, I was startled when the custodian lumbered by me with his oil can.

"You have a good summer, Miss," he mumbled as he crouched beside the front door aiming his can.

"You too," I answered, smiling. I straightened the paper button still pinned to my shirt, thinking that I just might keep it on all summer long.

I took one final look from the porch. The children were much farther in the distance by now, but I was still able to identify each of them by their unique silhouette. One by one, they fluttered down the street, around the corner, and out of sight.

I had forgotten to tell them that they were no longer wiggling little caterpillars. I had forgotten to tell them that throughout the year they had become beautiful dancing butterflies. But watching them, I realized that it didn't seem to matter that I hadn't told them. It didn't matter because it seemed that somehow they already knew.

12

A Chance Meeting

The first time I got the inkling that I was being followed, I was in the soup aisle. By the time I was picking peaches in the produce section, I was pretty sure. And when a child landed on top of my sneakers in frozen foods, I was completely sure.

"Hi, Miss Rizzo!" croaked a puberty-stricken voice before me. It was one of my former students. She had just thrown her little sister onto my shoes.

"Well, hello, Karen!" I greeted her, barely recognizing her. She had grown at least a foot since I had seen her last. Tall and gangly now, she was no longer the pudgy, short-haired little girl I remembered. But I noticed her deep almond eyes hadn't changed.

"Well, hello to you too!" I said down to my shoes. A smaller version of the same eyes peered up at me. The little girl said nothing. Instead, she plugged a thumb firmly into her mouth.

"UUUGGGH," groaned the big sister. "I can't believe she's still doing that. I keep telling her she CANNOT suck her thumb in kindergarten. She's going to be in your class next year!" she squealed. Her words rushed out of her mouth at a speed that only preteens can accomplish. Her voice got higher as she talked.

"Oh, I'm sure she'll do fine," I said, smiling down at her. Her thumb remained tightly plugged. "Actually, there's nothing to it," I said, repeating a phrase that I had long before prepared for nervous preschoolers. "First you'll color an apple, then you'll paste a turkey, next you'll glitter a Christmas tree, after that you'll draw a snowflake, then you'll cut a heart, after that you'll trace a shamrock, then you'll paint raindrops, next you'll glue flowers, and then you'll write good-bye. And after you do all of that, kindergarten will be over. There's really nothing to it." I shrugged.

"Bethie has braces and Jessie wears a bra," Karen announced in a hushed tone, catching me up on our mutual ten-year-old friends.

"Oh my!" I gasped, acting appropriately aghast. "These things happen, I guess," I said, enjoying my own touch of sarcasm, knowing she wouldn't notice. "Like I said," I repeated, gently taking the little one's hands and raising her to her feet, "I know you'll do fine." I smoothed her hair. "Actually, I'm sure you will because I think you probably already know everything you need to know to go to kindergarten."

I turned her sideways and peered into her right ear. "Yep," I nodded, turning her around and pulling the lobe of the other ear and looking in. "Oh, yes," I insisted. "Everything you need to know is already in there. You'll do great."

She unplugged her thumb and smiled broadly at me. She was incredibly cute. I poked her tummy. She giggled and replugged her thumb.

"OHHHH," Karen squealed. "There's Mom! We gotta go!" She screeched, grabbing her sister's hand and yanking her like a rag doll.

"'Bye, Miss Rizzo," she yelled, taking off like a bony-legged baby deer.

"Hey, what are you going to do in sixth grade?" I called to her.

"Probably die of embarrassment," she yelled over her shoulder back to me.

"Probably right." I laughed to myself, thinking that's usually the year for that kind of thing. "Good luck!" I called after her.

"Thanks," she said, disappearing out of sight.

As I tossed two packages of frozen peas into my cart, I suddenly felt anxious for school to start.

Journal